Chalk T

I had some yellow chalk,
so I drew the sun.

I had some green chalk,
so I drew the grass.

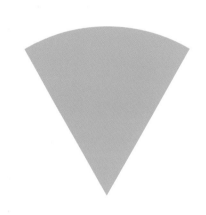

4

I had some blue chalk,
so I drew the sky.

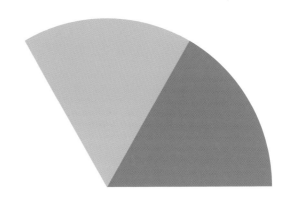

I had some purple chalk,
so I drew a house.

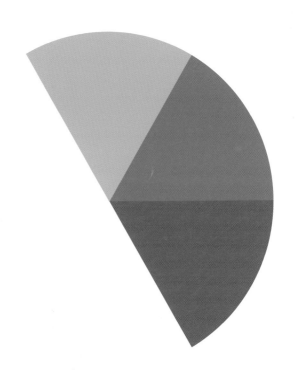

9

I had some red chalk,
so I drew some flowers.

11

I had some orange chalk,
so I drew a dog.

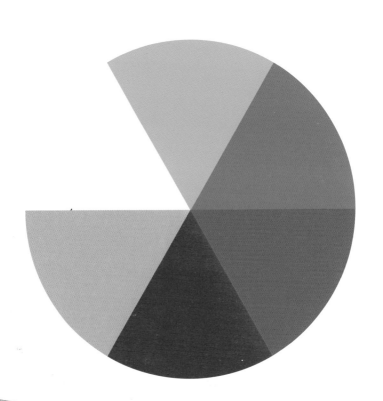

We had some chalk,
so we drew...

14

15

a picture.